Name

Date / /

Numbers
1 to 10

To parents: Write your child's name and the date above. Starting with this page, your child will practice reciting and writing numbers. Acquiring these skills will facilitate an understanding of addition. When your child completes each exercise, please offer lots of praise.

■ Draw a line from 1 to 5 in order while saying each number.

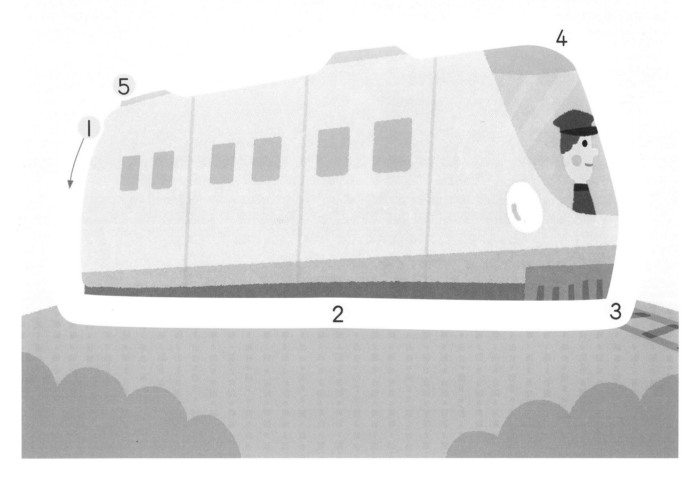

■ Trace the number in each box while saying each number.

| 1 | 2 | 3 | 4 | 5 | 6 | 7 | 8 | 9 | 10 |

■ Draw a line from 1 to 10 in order while saying each number.

■ Trace the number in each box while saying each number.

| 1 | 2 | 3 | 4 | 5 | 6 | 7 | 8 | 9 | 10 |

2 Numbers
1 to 15

Name

Date

/ /

To parents: When your child draws a line, it's okay if the line isn't perfectly straight. Make sure that your child is saying the numbers in the correct order while drawing the lines slowly and carefully.

■ Draw a line from 1 to 15 in order while saying each number.

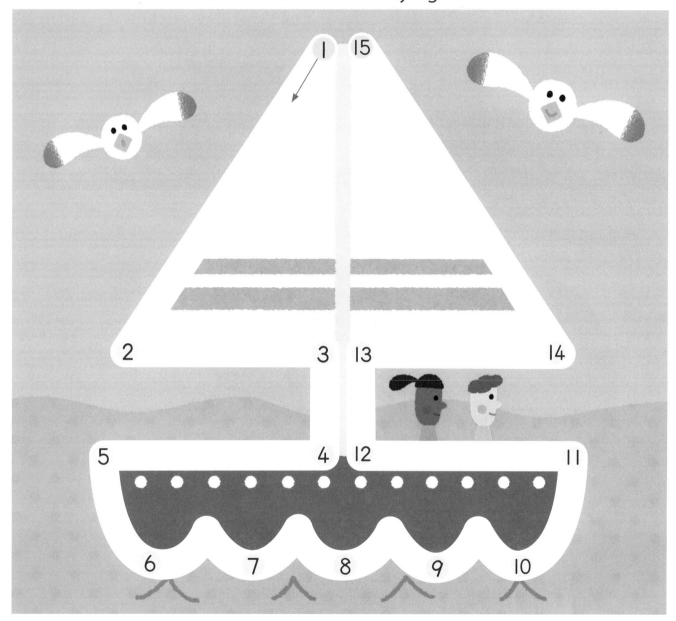

■ Trace the number in each box while saying each number.

1	2	3	4	5	6	7	8	9	10
11	12	13	14	15	16	17	18	19	20

■ Draw a line from 1 to 15 in order while saying each number.

■ Trace the number in each box while saying each number.

1	2	3	4	5	6	7	8	9	10
11	12	13	14	15	16	17	18	19	20

Numbers
1 to 20

Name

Date

/ /

To parents: Have your child say the numbers aloud while doing the exercise. Are they able to write from 1 to 20 easily?

■ Draw a line from 1 to 20 in order while saying each number.

■ Trace the number in each box while saying each number.

1	2	3	4	5	6	7	8	9	10
11	12	13	14	15	16	17	18	19	20

■ Draw a line from 1 to 20 in order while saying each number.

■ Trace the number in each box while saying each number.

1	2	3	4	5	6	7	8	9	10
11	12	13	14	15	16	17	18	19	20

Numbers
1 to 25

Name _____   Date ___ / ___ / ___

■ Draw a line from 1 to 25 in order while saying each number.

■ Trace the number in each box while saying each number.

11	12	13	14	15	16	17	18	19	20
21	22	23	24	25	26	27	28	29	30

■ Draw a line from 1 to 25 in order while saying each number.

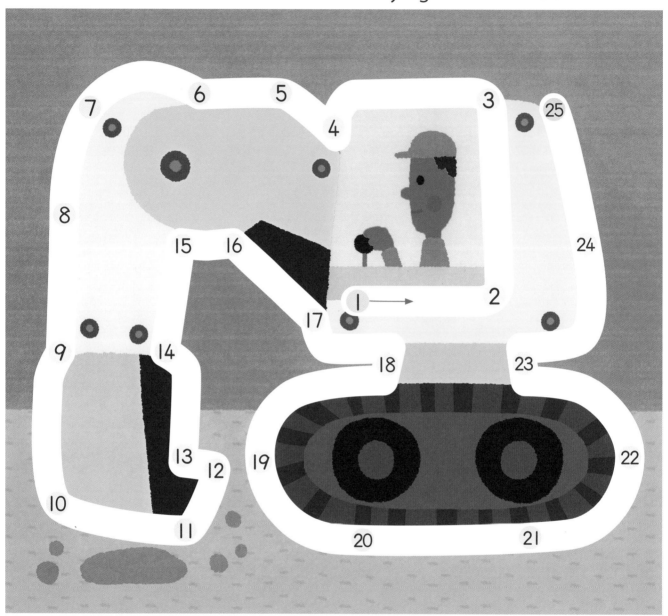

■ Trace the number in each box while saying each number.

11	12	13	14	15	16	17	18	19	20
21	22	23	24	25	26	27	28	29	30

Numbers
1 to 30

Name

Date   /   /

■ Draw a line from 1 to 30 in order while saying each number.

■ Trace the number in each box while saying each number.

11	12	13	14	15	16	17	18	19	20
21	22	23	24	25	26	27	28	29	30

■ Draw a line from 1 to 30 in order while saying each number.

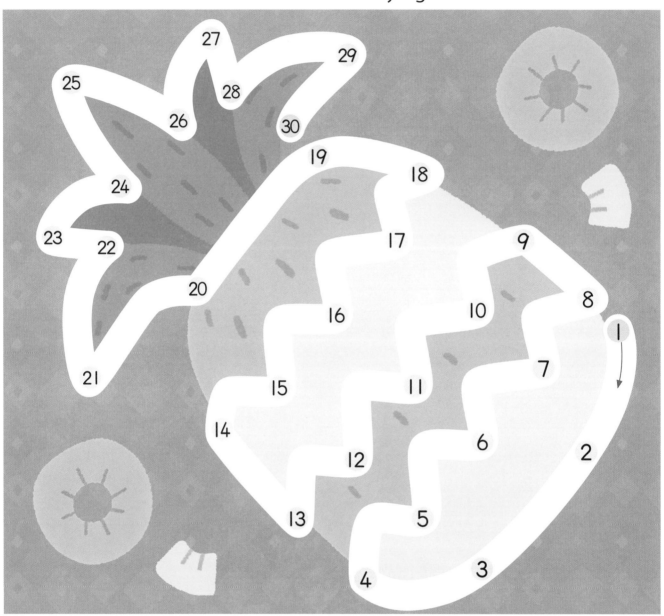

■ Trace the number in each box while saying each number.

11	12	13	14	15	16	17	18	19	20
21	22	23	24	25	26	27	28	29	30

Numbers
1 to 30

Name

Date
/ /

To parents: Has your child enjoyed learning so far? It is also a good idea for your child to write the numbers 1 to 30 on another piece of paper while saying them out loud.

■ Draw a line from 1 to 30 in order while saying each number.

■ Trace the number in each box while saying each number.

1	2	3	4	5	6	7	8	9	10
11	12	13	14	15	16	17	18	19	20
21	22	23	24	25	26	27	28	29	30

■ Draw a line from 1 to 30 in order while saying each number.

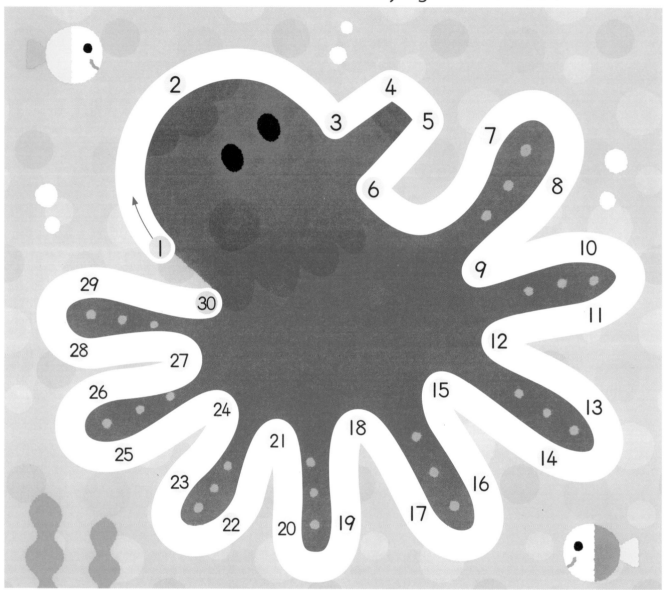

■ Trace the number in each box while saying each number.

1	2	3	4	5	6	7	8	9	10
11	12	13	14	15	16	17	18	19	20
21	22	23	24	25	26	27	28	29	30

Saying and Writing Numbers
1 to 10

Name

Date

/ /

To parents: Your child will practice writing numbers with the "next number" in mind, such as "the next number after 1 is 2", "the next number after 2 is 3", and so on. When your child can easily find the next number, they will be able to proceed with adding 1 smoothly.

■ Fill in the missing numbers. Say each number aloud.

| 1 | 2 | 3 | 4 | 5 | 6 | 7 | 8 | 9 | 10 |

| 1 | 2 | 3 | 4 | 5 | 6 | 7 | 8 | 9 | 10 |

| 1 | 2 | 3 | 4 | 5 | 6 | 7 | 8 | 9 | 10 |

| 1 | 2 | 3 | 4 | 5 | 6 | 7 | 8 | 9 | 10 |

| 1 | 2 | 3 | 4 | 5 | 6 | 7 | 8 | 9 | 10 |

■ Fill in the missing numbers. Say each number aloud.

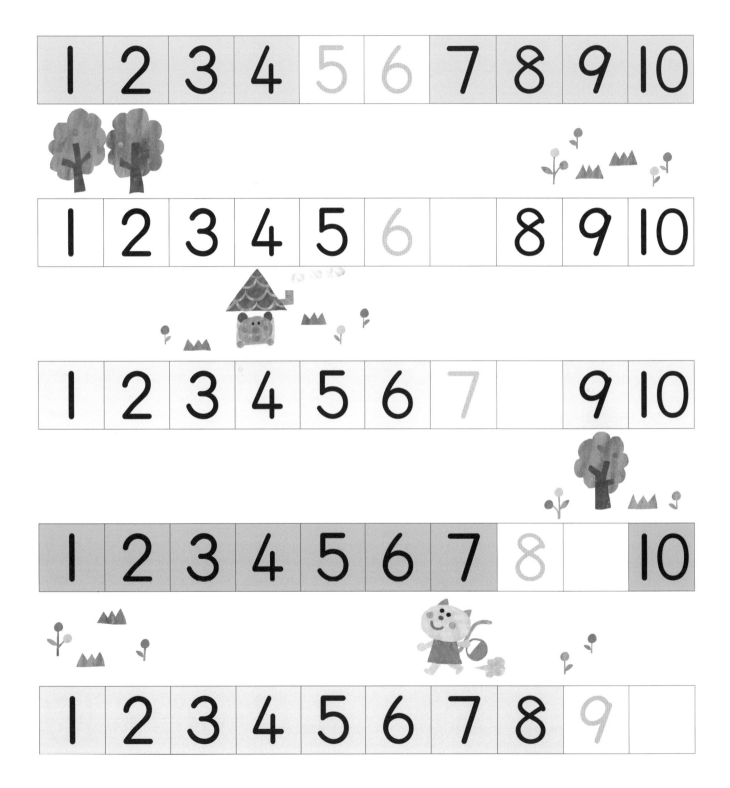

1 2 3 4 5 6 7 8 9 10

1 2 3 4 5 6 8 9 10

1 2 3 4 5 6 7 9 10

1 2 3 4 5 6 7 8 10

1 2 3 4 5 6 7 8 9

8 Saying and Writing Numbers
11 to 20

Name

Date

/ /

To parents: By reading the numbers in each chart out loud repeatedly, your child will become aware of the next number, which will help them learn adding 1 more smoothly.

■ Fill in the missing numbers. Say each number aloud.

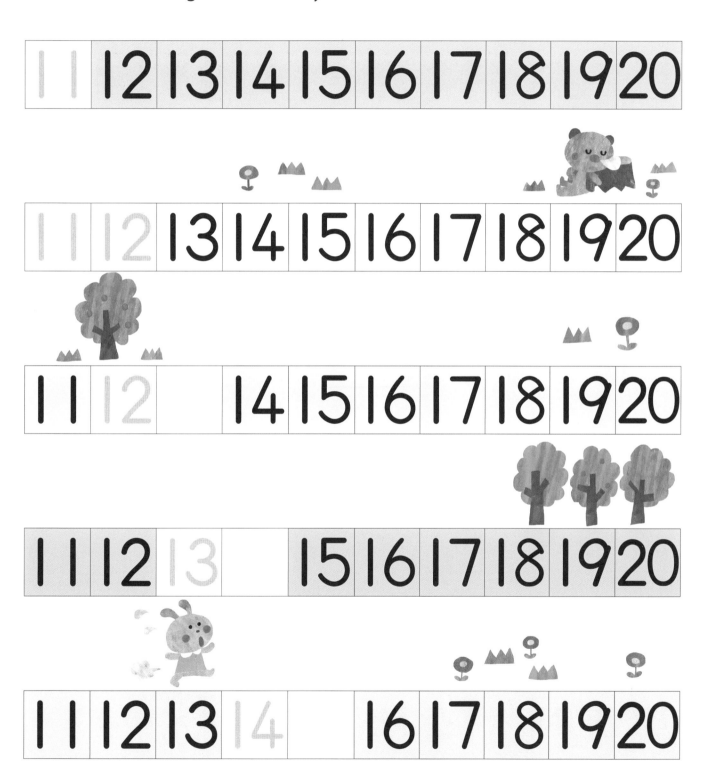

■ Fill in the missing numbers. Say each number aloud.

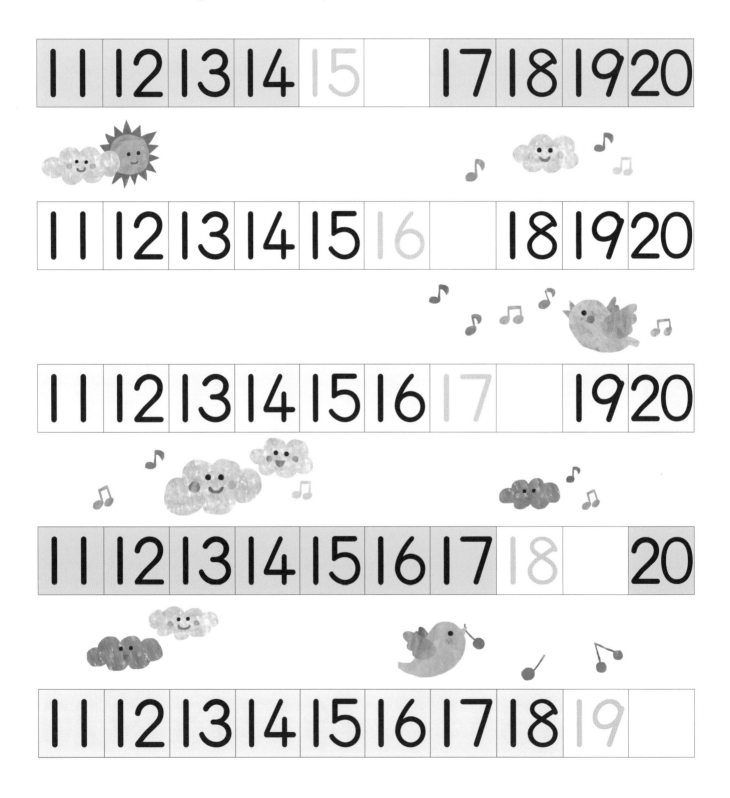

11 12 13 14 15 __ 17 18 19 20

11 12 13 14 15 16 __ 18 19 20

11 12 13 14 15 16 17 __ 19 20

11 12 13 14 15 16 17 18 __ 20

11 12 13 14 15 16 17 18 19

9 Saying and Writing Numbers
21 to 30

Name _____   Date ___/___/___

■ Fill in the missing numbers. Say each number aloud.

21 22 23 24 25 26 27 28 29 30

21 22 23 24 25 26 27 28 29 30

21 22 __ 24 25 26 27 28 29 30

21 22 23 __ 25 26 27 28 29 30

21 22 23 24 __ 26 27 28 29 30

■ Fill in the missing numbers. Say each number aloud.

21 22 23 24 25 __ 27 28 29 30

21 22 23 24 25 26 __ 28 29 30

21 22 23 24 25 26 27 __ 29 30

21 22 23 24 25 26 27 28 __ 30

21 22 23 24 25 26 27 28 29 __

Adding 1
1+1 to 9+1

Name

Date

/ /

To parents: Please use the number chart to make sure your child understands that when you add 1 to a number, the result will be the next number.

■ Fill in the missing numbers and then add the numbers below.

| 1 | 2 | 3 | 4 | 5 | 6 | 7 | 8 | 9 | 10 |

One Plus One Equals

$$1 + 1 = 2$$

Two Plus One Equals

$$2 + 1 = 3$$

| 1 | 2 | 3 | 4 | 5 | 6 | 7 | 8 | 9 | 10 |

Three Plus One Equals

$$3 + 1 = 4$$

Four Plus One Equals

$$4 + 1 = 5$$

| 1 | 2 | 3 | 4 | 5 | 6 | 7 | 8 | 9 | 10 |

Five Plus One Equals

$$5 + 1 = 6$$

Six Plus One Equals

$$6 + 1 = 7$$

■ Fill in the missing numbers and then add the numbers below.

| 1 | 2 | 3 | 4 | 5 | 6 | 7 | 8 | 9 | 10 |

Four Plus One Equals

$4 + 1 = 5$

Five Plus One Equals

$5 + 1 = 6$

| 1 | 2 | 3 | 4 | 5 | 6 | 7 | 8 | 9 | 10 |

Six Plus One Equals

$6 + 1 = 7$

Seven Plus One Equals

$7 + 1 = 8$

| 1 | 2 | 3 | 4 | 5 | 6 | 7 | 8 | 9 | 10 |

Eight Plus One Equals

$8 + 1 = 9$

Nine Plus One Equals

$9 + 1 = 10$

Adding 1
1+1 to 10+1

Name

Date
/ /

To parents: If your child seems to be having difficulty, you can say something like, "This is 2+1. What's the next number after 2?"

■ Fill in the missing numbers and then add the numbers below.

1	2	3	4	5	6	7	8	9	10

(1) 1 + 1 = 2

(2) 2 + 1 = 3

(3) 3 + 1 = 4

(4) 4 + 1 = 5

(5) 5 + 1 = 6

(6) 6 + 1 = 7

1	2	3	4	5	6	7	8	9	10

(7) 7 + 1 = 8

(8) 8 + 1 = 9

(9) 9 + 1 = 10

(10) 1 + 1 =

(11) 2 + 1 =

(12) 4 + 1 =

■ Fill in the missing numbers and then add the numbers below.

1	2	3	4	5	6	7	8	9	10

(1) $1 + 1 =$

(2) $3 + 1 =$

(3) $4 + 1 =$

(4) $6 + 1 =$

(5) $8 + 1 =$

(6) $9 + 1 =$

1	2			5		7		9	10
11	12	13	14	15	16	17	18	19	20

(7) $10 + 1 = 11$

(8) $2 + 1 =$

(9) $3 + 1 =$

(10) $5 + 1 =$

(11) $10 + 1 =$

(12) $7 + 1 =$

12 Adding 1
11+1 to 20+1

To parents: The concept of adding 1 is the same even when the starting number is larger. Have your child point to the number chart and check the next number.

■ Fill in the missing numbers and then add the numbers below.

| 11 | 12 | 13 | 14 | 15 | 16 | 17 | 18 | 19 | 20 |

(1) $11 + 1 = 12$

(4) $14 + 1 = 15$

(2) $12 + 1 = 13$

(5) $15 + 1 = 16$

(3) $13 + 1 = 14$

(6) $16 + 1 = 17$

| 11 | 12 | 13 | 14 | 15 | 16 | 17 | 18 | 19 | 20 |

(7) $17 + 1 = 18$

(10) $12 + 1 =$

(8) $18 + 1 = 19$

(11) $13 + 1 =$

(9) $19 + 1 = 20$

(12) $15 + 1 =$

■ Fill in the missing numbers and then add the numbers below.

11	12	13	14	15	16	17	18	19	20

(1) 11 + 1 =

(2) 12 + 1 =

(3) 14 + 1 =

(4) 16 + 1 =

(5) 17 + 1 =

(6) 19 + 1 =

11	12	13		15			18		20
21	22	23	24	25	26	27	28	29	30

(7) 20 + 1 = 21

(8) 13 + 1 =

(9) 15 + 1 =

(10) 18 + 1 =

(11) 16 + 1 =

(12) 20 + 1 =

Adding 1
21+1 to 29+1

Name

Date
/ /

To parents: If your child finds the same problem and copies the previous answer, don't worry. Knowing that it is the same problem and being able to find the answer is a good sign that your child's number recognition is improving. As they practice more, your child will learn to calculate better and they won't need to look at the previous answers.

■ Fill in the missing numbers and then add the numbers below.

21	22	23	24	25	26	27	28	29	30

(1) 21 + 1 = 22

(2) 22 + 1 = 23

(3) 23 + 1 = 24

(4) 24 + 1 = 25

(5) 25 + 1 = 26

(6) 26 + 1 = 27

21	22	23	24	25	26	27	28	29	30

(7) 27 + 1 = 28

(8) 28 + 1 = 29

(9) 29 + 1 = 30

(10) 21 + 1 =

(11) 23 + 1 =

(12) 24 + 1 =

25

■ Fill in the missing numbers and then add the numbers below.

21	22	23	24	25	26	27	28	29	30

(1) 21 + 1 =

(2) 22 + 1 =

(3) 24 + 1 =

(4) 25 + 1 =

(5) 27 + 1 =

(6) 29 + 1 =

21					26			

(7) 24 + 1 =

(8) 21 + 1 =

(9) 27 + 1 =

(10) 22 + 1 =

(11) 23 + 1 =

(12) 29 + 1 =

(13) 26 + 1 =

(14) 28 + 1 =

14 Adding 1
1+1 to 5+1

Name

Date

/ /

To parents: After your child finishes one sheet, please check the answers. If your child seems to have made a mistake in the answer, ask them to think again. If your child gets all the answers correct, please offer lots of praise.

■ Add.

(1) $1 + 1 = 2$

(2) $2 + 1 = 3$

(3) $3 + 1 = 4$

(4) $1 + 1 =$

(5) $3 + 1 =$

(6) $2 + 1 =$

(7) $3 + 1 =$

(8) $2 + 1 =$

(9) $1 + 1 =$

(10) $3 + 1 =$

(11) $1 + 1 =$

(12) $2 + 1 =$

(13) $1 + 1 =$

(14) $2 + 1 =$

(15) $3 + 1 =$

(16) $2 + 1 =$

(17) $3 + 1 =$

(18) $1 + 1 =$

(19) $2 + 1 =$

(20) $1 + 1 =$

| 1 | 2 | 3 | 4 | 5 | 6 | 7 | 8 | 9 | 10 |

■ Add.

(1) $2 + 1 =$ (11) $1 + 1 =$

(2) $1 + 1 =$ (12) $2 + 1 =$

(3) $3 + 1 =$ (13) $4 + 1 =$

(4) $4 + 1 =$ (14) $5 + 1 =$

(5) $5 + 1 =$ (15) $3 + 1 =$

(6) $1 + 1 =$ (16) $2 + 1 =$

(7) $3 + 1 =$ (17) $5 + 1 =$

(8) $2 + 1 =$ (18) $1 + 1 =$

(9) $4 + 1 =$ (19) $3 + 1 =$

(10) $5 + 1 =$ (20) $4 + 1 =$

1	2	3	4	5	6	7	8	9	10

15 Adding 1
1+1 to 9+1

Name

Date

/ /

To parents: Learning to add 1 is a basic step towards successfully understanding addition. Starting with this page, your child will repeatedly practice problems that include the number 1 in order to gain solid calculation abilities. If your child needs a hint, tell them to look at the number chart on the bottom of each page for the correct answer.

■ Add.

(1) $3 + 1 =$

(2) $1 + 1 =$

(3) $2 + 1 =$

(4) $4 + 1 =$

(5) $5 + 1 =$

(6) $6 + 1 =$

(7) $7 + 1 =$

(8) $8 + 1 =$

(9) $9 + 1 =$

(10) $1 + 1 =$

(11) $2 + 1 =$

(12) $4 + 1 =$

(13) $3 + 1 =$

(14) $5 + 1 =$

(15) $6 + 1 =$

(16) $8 + 1 =$

(17) $9 + 1 =$

(18) $7 + 1 =$

(19) $1 + 1 =$

(20) $6 + 1 =$

| 1 | 2 | 3 | 4 | 5 | 6 | 7 | 8 | 9 | 10 |

■ Add.

(1) $1 + 1 =$

(2) $4 + 1 =$

(3) $2 + 1 =$

(4) $3 + 1 =$

(5) $5 + 1 =$

(6) $7 + 1 =$

(7) $6 + 1 =$

(8) $8 + 1 =$

(9) $9 + 1 =$

(10) $3 + 1 =$

(11) $5 + 1 =$

(12) $6 + 1 =$

(13) $8 + 1 =$

(14) $7 + 1 =$

(15) $9 + 1 =$

(16) $2 + 1 =$

(17) $1 + 1 =$

(18) $3 + 1 =$

(19) $5 + 1 =$

(20) $4 + 1 =$

| 1 | 2 | 3 | 4 | 5 | 6 | 7 | 8 | 9 | 10 |

Adding 1
1+1 to 14+1

Name

Date
/ /

To parents: It takes a lot of concentration for your child to practice 40 addition problems on one sheet. If your child is having trouble concentrating, it is okay to take a break.

■ Add.

(1) $2 + 1 =$

(2) $3 + 1 =$

(3) $1 + 1 =$

(4) $4 + 1 =$

(5) $6 + 1 =$

(6) $5 + 1 =$

(7) $7 + 1 =$

(8) $8 + 1 =$

(9) $9 + 1 =$

(10) $10 + 1 =$

(11) $11 + 1 =$

(12) $12 + 1 =$

(13) $13 + 1 =$

(14) $14 + 1 =$

(15) $10 + 1 =$

(16) $11 + 1 =$

(17) $13 + 1 =$

(18) $14 + 1 =$

(19) $12 + 1 =$

(20) $10 + 1 =$

| 1 | 2 | 3 | 4 | 5 | 6 | 7 | 8 | 9 | 10 | 11 | 12 | 13 | 14 | 15 | 16 | 17 | 18 | 19 | 20 |

■Add.

(1)　6 + 1 =

(2)　5 + 1 =

(3)　7 + 1 =

(4)　9 + 1 =

(5)　10 + 1 =

(6)　12 + 1 =

(7)　8 + 1 =

(8)　11 + 1 =

(9)　13 + 1 =

(10)　14 + 1 =

(11)　7 + 1 =

(12)　10 + 1 =

(13)　5 + 1 =

(14)　8 + 1 =

(15)　11 + 1 =

(16)　14 + 1 =

(17)　6 + 1 =

(18)　12 + 1 =

(19)　9 + 1 =

(20)　13 + 1 =

1	2	3	4	5	6	7	8	9	10	11	12	13	14	15	16	17	18	19	20

Adding 1
10+1 to 19+1

■Add.

(1)　10 + 1 =

(2)　12 + 1 =

(3)　11 + 1 =

(4)　13 + 1 =

(5)　14 + 1 =

(6)　15 + 1 =

(7)　17 + 1 =

(8)　16 + 1 =

(9)　18 + 1 =

(10)　19 + 1 =

(11)　12 + 1 =

(12)　11 + 1 =

(13)　10 + 1 =

(14)　13 + 1 =

(15)　15 + 1 =

(16)　16 + 1 =

(17)　14 + 1 =

(18)　17 + 1 =

(19)　19 + 1 =

(20)　18 + 1 =

| 1 | 2 | 3 | 4 | 5 | 6 | 7 | 8 | 9 | 10 | 11 | 12 | 13 | 14 | 15 | 16 | 17 | 18 | 19 | 20 |

■ Add.

(1) $12 + 1 =$

(2) $10 + 1 =$

(3) $13 + 1 =$

(4) $11 + 1 =$

(5) $14 + 1 =$

(6) $15 + 1 =$

(7) $18 + 1 =$

(8) $17 + 1 =$

(9) $19 + 1 =$

(10) $16 + 1 =$

(11) $14 + 1 =$

(12) $11 + 1 =$

(13) $17 + 1 =$

(14) $15 + 1 =$

(15) $13 + 1 =$

(16) $18 + 1 =$

(17) $16 + 1 =$

(18) $10 + 1 =$

(19) $19 + 1 =$

(20) $12 + 1 =$

| 1 | 2 | 3 | 4 | 5 | 6 | 7 | 8 | 9 | 10 | 11 | 12 | 13 | 14 | 15 | 16 | 17 | 18 | 19 | 20 |

18 Adding 1
1+1 to 19+1

■ Add.

(1) 1 + 1 =

(2) 2 + 1 =

(3) 4 + 1 =

(4) 5 + 1 =

(5) 3 + 1 =

(6) 6 + 1 =

(7) 8 + 1 =

(8) 7 + 1 =

(9) 9 + 1 =

(10) 10 + 1 =

(11) 12 + 1 =

(12) 13 + 1 =

(13) 11 + 1 =

(14) 14 + 1 =

(15) 15 + 1 =

(16) 17 + 1 =

(17) 19 + 1 =

(18) 18 + 1 =

(19) 16 + 1 =

(20) 11 + 1 =

1	2	3	4	5	6	7	8	9	10	11	12	13	14	15	16	17	18	19	20

■ Add.

(1) 4 + 1 =

(2) 7 + 1 =

(3) 13 + 1 =

(4) 1 + 1 =

(5) 12 + 1 =

(6) 15 + 1 =

(7) 3 + 1 =

(8) 11 + 1 =

(9) 18 + 1 =

(10) 8 + 1 =

(11) 10 + 1 =

(12) 5 + 1 =

(13) 17 + 1 =

(14) 11 + 1 =

(15) 6 + 1 =

(16) 19 + 1 =

(17) 2 + 1 =

(18) 16 + 1 =

(19) 9 + 1 =

(20) 14 + 1 =

| 1 | 2 | 3 | 4 | 5 | 6 | 7 | 8 | 9 | 10 | 11 | 12 | 13 | 14 | 15 | 16 | 17 | 18 | 19 | 20 |

19 Adding 1
15+1 to 29+1

■Add.

(1) 17 + 1 =

(2) 15 + 1 =

(3) 16 + 1 =

(4) 18 + 1 =

(5) 19 + 1 =

(6) 20 + 1 =

(7) 21 + 1 =

(8) 22 + 1 =

(9) 23 + 1 =

(10) 24 + 1 =

(11) 20 + 1 =

(12) 21 + 1 =

(13) 23 + 1 =

(14) 22 + 1 =

(15) 24 + 1 =

(16) 21 + 1 =

(17) 22 + 1 =

(18) 20 + 1 =

(19) 24 + 1 =

(20) 23 + 1 =

| 11 | 12 | 13 | 14 | 15 | 16 | 17 | 18 | 19 | 20 | 21 | 22 | 23 | 24 | 25 | 26 | 27 | 28 | 29 | 30 |

■Add.

(1) 20 + 1 =

(2) 22 + 1 =

(3) 21 + 1 =

(4) 23 + 1 =

(5) 24 + 1 =

(6) 25 + 1 =

(7) 26 + 1 =

(8) 27 + 1 =

(9) 28 + 1 =

(10) 29 + 1 =

(11) 25 + 1 =

(12) 27 + 1 =

(13) 28 + 1 =

(14) 26 + 1 =

(15) 29 + 1 =

(16) 27 + 1 =

(17) 25 + 1 =

(18) 29 + 1 =

(19) 28 + 1 =

(20) 26 + 1 =

| 11 | 12 | 13 | 14 | 15 | 16 | 17 | 18 | 19 | 20 | 21 | 22 | 23 | 24 | 25 | 26 | 27 | 28 | 29 | 30 |

Adding 1
20+1 to 29+1

■ Add.

(1) 20 + 1 =

(2) 21 + 1 =

(3) 22 + 1 =

(4) 24 + 1 =

(5) 23 + 1 =

(6) 25 + 1 =

(7) 26 + 1 =

(8) 29 + 1 =

(9) 27 + 1 =

(10) 28 + 1 =

(11) 21 + 1 =

(12) 23 + 1 =

(13) 20 + 1 =

(14) 22 + 1 =

(15) 25 + 1 =

(16) 24 + 1 =

(17) 28 + 1 =

(18) 26 + 1 =

(19) 27 + 1 =

(20) 29 + 1 =

| 11 | 12 | 13 | 14 | 15 | 16 | 17 | 18 | 19 | 20 | 21 | 22 | 23 | 24 | 25 | 26 | 27 | 28 | 29 | 30 |

■ Add.

(1) 24 + 1 =

(2) 21 + 1 =

(3) 28 + 1 =

(4) 25 + 1 =

(5) 29 + 1 =

(6) 22 + 1 =

(7) 26 + 1 =

(8) 20 + 1 =

(9) 23 + 1 =

(10) 27 + 1 =

(11) 25 + 1 =

(12) 29 + 1 =

(13) 21 + 1 =

(14) 24 + 1 =

(15) 20 + 1 =

(16) 27 + 1 =

(17) 23 + 1 =

(18) 28 + 1 =

(19) 26 + 1 =

(20) 22 + 1 =

| 11 | 12 | 13 | 14 | 15 | 16 | 17 | 18 | 19 | 20 | 21 | 22 | 23 | 24 | 25 | 26 | 27 | 28 | 29 | 30 |

21 Adding 1
1+1 to 29+1

Name

Date　　/　/

To parents: If your child is able to do addition easily, you may want to make some additional adding 1 problems and give them to your child.

■ Add.

(1)　　1 + 1 =

(2)　　2 + 1 =

(3)　　3 + 1 =

(4)　　5 + 1 =

(5)　　7 + 1 =

(6)　　8 + 1 =

(7)　10 + 1 =

(8)　11 + 1 =

(9)　13 + 1 =

(10)　14 + 1 =

(11)　　6 + 1 =

(12)　　5 + 1 =

(13)　12 + 1 =

(14)　14 + 1 =

(15)　　3 + 1 =

(16)　10 + 1 =

(17)　　9 + 1 =

(18)　　4 + 1 =

(19)　　1 + 1 =

(20)　11 + 1 =

| 1 | 2 | 3 | 4 | 5 | 6 | 7 | 8 | 9 | 10 | 11 | 12 | 13 | 14 | 15 | 16 | 17 | 18 | 19 | 20 |

■ Add.

(1) 16 + 1 =

(2) 17 + 1 =

(3) 19 + 1 =

(4) 20 + 1 =

(5) 21 + 1 =

(6) 23 + 1 =

(7) 24 + 1 =

(8) 26 + 1 =

(9) 28 + 1 =

(10) 29 + 1 =

(11) 19 + 1 =

(12) 22 + 1 =

(13) 27 + 1 =

(14) 15 + 1 =

(15) 18 + 1 =

(16) 25 + 1 =

(17) 29 + 1 =

(18) 16 + 1 =

(19) 20 + 1 =

(20) 24 + 1 =

| 11 | 12 | 13 | 14 | 15 | 16 | 17 | 18 | 19 | 20 | 21 | 22 | 23 | 24 | 25 | 26 | 27 | 28 | 29 | 30 |

22 Saying and Writing Numbers
1 to 15

Name

Date

/ /

To parents: Your child will practice writing numbers with the "number after the next number" in mind. When your child can easily find the number after the next number, they will be able to proceed with adding 2 smoothly.

■ Fill in the missing numbers. Say each number aloud.

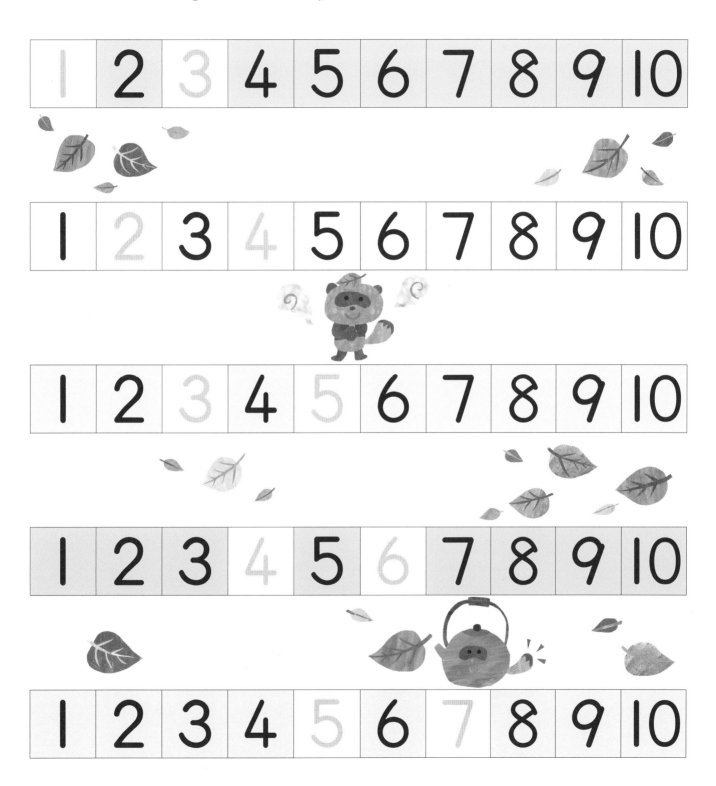

■ Fill in the missing numbers. Say each number aloud.

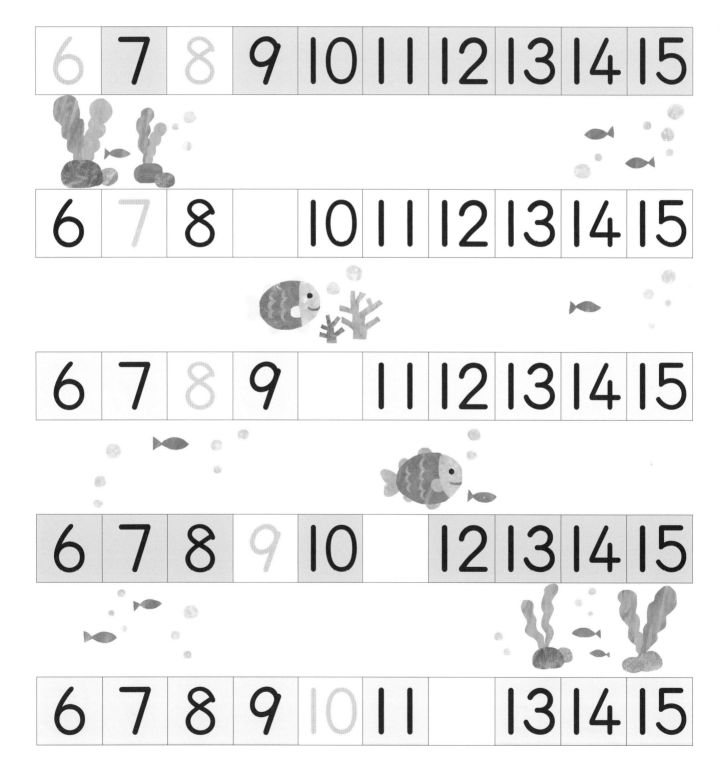

6 7 8 9 10 11 12 13 14 15

6 7 8 10 11 12 13 14 15

6 7 8 9 11 12 13 14 15

6 7 8 9 10 12 13 14 15

6 7 8 9 10 11 13 14 15

23 Saying and Writing Numbers
11 to 25

Name _____ Date __/__/__

■ Fill in the missing numbers. Say each number aloud.

| 11 | 12 | 13 | 14 | 15 | 16 | 17 | 18 | 19 | 20 |

| 11 | 12 | 13 | | 15 | 16 | 17 | 18 | 19 | 20 |

| 11 | 12 | 13 | 14 | | 16 | 17 | 18 | 19 | 20 |

| 11 | 12 | 13 | 14 | 15 | | 17 | 18 | 19 | 20 |

| 11 | 12 | 13 | 14 | 15 | 16 | | 18 | 19 | 20 |

45

■ Fill in the missing numbers. Say each number aloud.

| 16 | 17 | 18 | 19 | 20 | 21 | 22 | 23 | 24 | 25 |

| 16 | 17 | 18 | | 20 | 21 | 22 | 23 | 24 | 25 |

| 16 | 17 | 18 | 19 | | 21 | 22 | 23 | 24 | 25 |

| 16 | 17 | 18 | 19 | 20 | | 22 | 23 | 24 | 25 |

| 16 | 17 | 18 | 19 | 20 | 21 | | 23 | 24 | 25 |

24 Saying and Writing Numbers
21 to 35

Name

Date

/ /

■ Fill in the missing numbers. Say each number aloud.

21 **22** 23 **24 25 26 27 28 29 30**

21 22 **23** **25 26 27 28 29 30**

21 22 23 **24** **26 27 28 29 30**

21 22 23 24 **25** **27 28 29 30**

21 22 23 24 25 **26** **28 29 30**

47

■ Fill in the missing numbers. Say each number aloud.

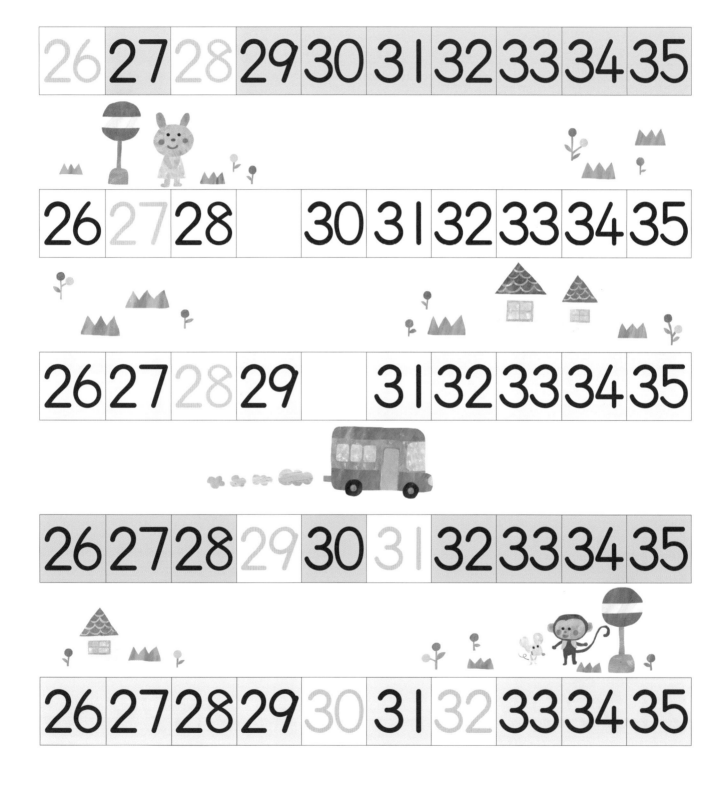

26 27 28 29 30 31 32 33 34 35

26 27 28   30 31 32 33 34 35

26 27 28 29   31 32 33 34 35

26 27 28 29 30 31 32 33 34 35

26 27 28 29 30 31 32 33 34 35

Adding 2
1+2 to 8+2

To parents: Please use the number chart to make sure your child understands that when you add 2 to a number, the result will be the number after the next number.

■ Fill in the missing numbers and then add the numbers below.

| 1 | 2 | 3 | 4 | 5 | 6 | 7 | 8 | 9 | 10 |

One   Plus   Two   Equals

$1 + 2 = 3$

Two   Plus   Two   Equals

$2 + 2 = 4$

| 1 | 2 | 3 | 4 | 5 | 6 | 7 | 8 | 9 | 10 |

Three   Plus   Two   Equals

$3 + 2 = 5$

Four   Plus   Two   Equals

$4 + 2 = 6$

| 1 | 2 | 3 | 4 | 5 | 6 | 7 | 8 | 9 | 10 |

Five   Plus   Two   Equals

$5 + 2 = 7$

Six   Plus   Two   Equals

$6 + 2 = 8$

■ Fill in the missing numbers and then add the numbers below.

| 1 | 2 | 3 | 4 | 5 | 6 | 7 | 8 | 9 | 10 |

Three Plus Two Equals
$$3 + 2 = 5$$

Four Plus Two Equals
$$4 + 2 = 6$$

| 1 | 2 | 3 | 4 | 5 | 6 | 7 | 8 | 9 | 10 |

Five Plus Two Equals
$$5 + 2 = 7$$

Six Plus Two Equals
$$6 + 2 = 8$$

| 1 | 2 | 3 | 4 | 5 | 6 | 7 | 8 | 9 | 10 |

Seven Plus Two Equals
$$7 + 2 = 9$$

Eight Plus Two Equals
$$8 + 2 = 10$$

26 Adding 2
1+2 to 10+2

■ Fill in the missing numbers and then add the numbers below.

| 1 | 2 | 3 | 4 | 5 | 6 | 7 | 8 | 9 | 10 |

(1) $1 + 2 = 3$

(2) $2 + 2 = 4$

(3) $3 + 2 = 5$

(4) $4 + 2 = 6$

(5) $5 + 2 = 7$

(6) $6 + 2 = 8$

| 1 | 2 | 3 | 4 | 5 | 6 | 7 | 8 | 9 | 10 |

(7) $7 + 2 = 9$

(8) $8 + 2 = 10$

(9) $1 + 2 =$

(10) $2 + 2 =$

(11) $4 + 2 =$

(12) $5 + 2 =$

■ Fill in the missing numbers and then add the numbers below.

1	2	3	4	5	6	7	8	9	10

(1)　1 + 2 =

(2)　3 + 2 =

(3)　4 + 2 =

(4)　5 + 2 =

(5)　6 + 2 =

(6)　8 + 2 =

1	2	3		5	6	7	8		10
11	12	13	14	15	16	17	18	19	20

(7)　9 + 2 = 11

(8)　10 + 2 = 12

(9)　2 + 2 =

(10)　10 + 2 =

(11)　7 + 2 =

(12)　9 + 2 =

52

Adding 2
11+2 to 20+2

To parents: The concept of adding 2 is the same even when the starting number is larger. Have your child point to the number chart and check the number after the next number.

■ Fill in the missing numbers and then add the numbers below.

11	12	13	14	15	16	17	18	19	20

(1) $11 + 2 = 13$

(2) $12 + 2 = 14$

(3) $13 + 2 = 15$

(4) $14 + 2 = 16$

(5) $15 + 2 = 17$

(6) $16 + 2 = 18$

11	12	13	14	15	16	17	18	19	20

(7) $17 + 2 = 19$

(8) $18 + 2 = 20$

(9) $11 + 2 =$

(10) $13 + 2 =$

(11) $14 + 2 =$

(12) $16 + 2 =$

53

■ Fill in the missing numbers and then add the numbers below.

11	12	13	14	15	16	17	18	19	20

(1) $11 + 2 =$

(2) $13 + 2 =$

(3) $14 + 2 =$

(4) $15 + 2 =$

(5) $17 + 2 =$

(6) $18 + 2 =$

11	12	13		15	16	17		19	20
21	22	23	24	25	26	27	28	29	30

(7) $19 + 2 = 21$

(8) $20 + 2 = 22$

(9) $16 + 2 =$

(10) $12 + 2 =$

(11) $19 + 2 =$

(12) $20 + 2 =$

Adding 2
21+2 to 28+2

■ Fill in the missing numbers and then add the numbers below.

| 21 | 22 | 23 | 24 | 25 | 26 | 27 | 28 | 29 | 30 |

(1) $21 + 2 = 23$

(2) $22 + 2 = 24$

(3) $23 + 2 = 25$

(4) $24 + 2 = 26$

(5) $25 + 2 = 27$

(6) $26 + 2 = 28$

| 21 | 22 | 23 | 24 | 25 | 26 | 27 | 28 | 29 | 30 |

(7) $27 + 2 = 29$

(8) $28 + 2 = 30$

(9) $21 + 2 =$

(10) $22 + 2 =$

(11) $23 + 2 =$

(12) $25 + 2 =$

■ Fill in the missing numbers and then add the numbers below.

21	22	23	24	25	26	27	28	29	30

(1) 21 + 2 =

(2) 22 + 2 =

(3) 24 + 2 =

(4) 25 + 2 =

(5) 26 + 2 =

(6) 28 + 2 =

21	22								

(7) 26 + 2 =

(8) 23 + 2 =

(9) 24 + 2 =

(10) 22 + 2 =

(11) 28 + 2 =

(12) 21 + 2 =

(13) 27 + 2 =

(14) 25 + 2 =

Adding 2
1+2 to 5+2

Name

Date

/ /

■ Add.

(1)　1 + 2 = 3

(2)　2 + 2 = 4

(3)　3 + 2 = 5

(4)　2 + 2 =

(5)　3 + 2 =

(6)　1 + 2 =

(7)　2 + 2 =

(8)　1 + 2 =

(9)　3 + 2 =

(10)　1 + 2 =

(11)　2 + 2 =

(12)　3 + 2 =

(13)　2 + 2 =

(14)　1 + 2 =

(15)　3 + 2 =

(16)　1 + 2 =

(17)　3 + 2 =

(18)　2 + 2 =

(19)　3 + 2 =

(20)　2 + 2 =

| 1 | 2 | 3 | 4 | 5 | 6 | 7 | 8 | 9 | 10 |

■ Add.

(1) 2 + 2 =

(2) 1 + 2 =

(3) 3 + 2 =

(4) 4 + 2 =

(5) 5 + 2 =

(6) 1 + 2 =

(7) 3 + 2 =

(8) 4 + 2 =

(9) 5 + 2 =

(10) 2 + 2 =

(11) 1 + 2 =

(12) 3 + 2 =

(13) 2 + 2 =

(14) 4 + 2 =

(15) 5 + 2 =

(16) 3 + 2 =

(17) 5 + 2 =

(18) 1 + 2 =

(19) 2 + 2 =

(20) 4 + 2 =

| 1 | 2 | 3 | 4 | 5 | 6 | 7 | 8 | 9 | 10 |

Adding 2
1+2 to 8+2

To parents: There is number chart at the bottom of each page of this section. Use it to give your child a hint that the answers are included in the chart.

■ Add.

(1)   1 + 2 =

(2)   3 + 2 =

(3)   2 + 2 =

(4)   4 + 2 =

(5)   5 + 2 =

(6)   6 + 2 =

(7)   7 + 2 =

(8)   8 + 2 =

(9)   1 + 2 =

(10)   2 + 2 =

(11)   4 + 2 =

(12)   3 + 2 =

(13)   5 + 2 =

(14)   6 + 2 =

(15)   8 + 2 =

(16)   7 + 2 =

(17)   3 + 2 =

(18)   2 + 2 =

(19)   4 + 2 =

(20)   7 + 2 =

1	2	3	4	5	6	7	8	9	10

■Add.

(1) 2 + 2 =

(2) 3 + 2 =

(3) 1 + 2 =

(4) 4 + 2 =

(5) 5 + 2 =

(6) 7 + 2 =

(7) 6 + 2 =

(8) 8 + 2 =

(9) 3 + 2 =

(10) 5 + 2 =

(11) 6 + 2 =

(12) 4 + 2 =

(13) 7 + 2 =

(14) 2 + 2 =

(15) 5 + 2 =

(16) 1 + 2 =

(17) 8 + 2 =

(18) 3 + 2 =

(19) 7 + 2 =

(20) 4 + 2 =

| 1 | 2 | 3 | 4 | 5 | 6 | 7 | 8 | 9 | 10 |

Adding 2
1+2 to 13+2

Name

Date

/ /

To parents: In order to understand the concept of adding 2, it is important that your child master number recitation and the ability to add 1 first. If they are having difficulty, please return to the section on adding 1.

■Add.

(1) $3 + 2 =$

(2) $4 + 2 =$

(3) $1 + 2 =$

(4) $6 + 2 =$

(5) $2 + 2 =$

(6) $5 + 2 =$

(7) $7 + 2 =$

(8) $8 + 2 =$

(9) $9 + 2 =$

(10) $10 + 2 =$

(11) $11 + 2 =$

(12) $12 + 2 =$

(13) $13 + 2 =$

(14) $9 + 2 =$

(15) $10 + 2 =$

(16) $12 + 2 =$

(17) $13 + 2 =$

(18) $11 + 2 =$

(19) $10 + 2 =$

(20) $9 + 2 =$

| 1 | 2 | 3 | 4 | 5 | 6 | 7 | 8 | 9 | 10 | 11 | 12 | 13 | 14 | 15 | 16 | 17 | 18 | 19 | 20 |

■Add.

(1) 5 + 2 =

(2) 4 + 2 =

(3) 7 + 2 =

(4) 8 + 2 =

(5) 6 + 2 =

(6) 10 + 2 =

(7) 11 + 2 =

(8) 9 + 2 =

(9) 12 + 2 =

(10) 13 + 2 =

(11) 8 + 2 =

(12) 10 + 2 =

(13) 11 + 2 =

(14) 4 + 2 =

(15) 9 + 2 =

(16) 5 + 2 =

(17) 13 + 2 =

(18) 6 + 2 =

(19) 12 + 2 =

(20) 7 + 2 =

| 1 | 2 | 3 | 4 | 5 | 6 | 7 | 8 | 9 | 10 | 11 | 12 | 13 | 14 | 15 | 16 | 17 | 18 | 19 | 20 |

 **Adding 2**
9+2 to 18+2

To parents: It takes a lot of concentration for your child to practice 40 addition problems in one sitting. If your child is having trouble concentrating, it is okay to take a break.

■ Add.

(1) $10 + 2 =$

(2) $11 + 2 =$

(3) $9 + 2 =$

(4) $12 + 2 =$

(5) $13 + 2 =$

(6) $14 + 2 =$

(7) $15 + 2 =$

(8) $16 + 2 =$

(9) $17 + 2 =$

(10) $18 + 2 =$

(11) $11 + 2 =$

(12) $12 + 2 =$

(13) $9 + 2 =$

(14) $10 + 2 =$

(15) $14 + 2 =$

(16) $13 + 2 =$

(17) $15 + 2 =$

(18) $16 + 2 =$

(19) $18 + 2 =$

(20) $17 + 2 =$

1	2	3	4	5	6	7	8	9	10	11	12	13	14	15	16	17	18	19	20

■Add.

(1) $14 + 2 =$

(2) $17 + 2 =$

(3) $9 + 2 =$

(4) $15 + 2 =$

(5) $10 + 2 =$

(6) $11 + 2 =$

(7) $16 + 2 =$

(8) $12 + 2 =$

(9) $18 + 2 =$

(10) $13 + 2 =$

(11) $10 + 2 =$

(12) $17 + 2 =$

(13) $14 + 2 =$

(14) $12 + 2 =$

(15) $18 + 2 =$

(16) $13 + 2 =$

(17) $9 + 2 =$

(18) $15 + 2 =$

(19) $11 + 2 =$

(20) $16 + 2 =$

| 1 | 2 | 3 | 4 | 5 | 6 | 7 | 8 | 9 | 10 | 11 | 12 | 13 | 14 | 15 | 16 | 17 | 18 | 19 | 20 |

Adding 2

1+2 to 18+2

■ Add.

(1) 1 + 2 =

(2) 2 + 2 =

(3) 4 + 2 =

(4) 3 + 2 =

(5) 5 + 2 =

(6) 6 + 2 =

(7) 8 + 2 =

(8) 7 + 2 =

(9) 10 + 2 =

(10) 11 + 2 =

(11) 9 + 2 =

(12) 12 + 2 =

(13) 14 + 2 =

(14) 15 + 2 =

(15) 13 + 2 =

(16) 16 + 2 =

(17) 18 + 2 =

(18) 17 + 2 =

(19) 3 + 2 =

(20) 8 + 2 =

| 1 | 2 | 3 | 4 | 5 | 6 | 7 | 8 | 9 | 10 | 11 | 12 | 13 | 14 | 15 | 16 | 17 | 18 | 19 | 20 |

■Add.

(1) $6 + 2 =$

(2) $11 + 2 =$

(3) $15 + 2 =$

(4) $4 + 2 =$

(5) $18 + 2 =$

(6) $16 + 2 =$

(7) $7 + 2 =$

(8) $12 + 2 =$

(9) $9 + 2 =$

(10) $3 + 2 =$

(11) $14 + 2 =$

(12) $5 + 2 =$

(13) $8 + 2 =$

(14) $1 + 2 =$

(15) $17 + 2 =$

(16) $13 + 2 =$

(17) $2 + 2 =$

(18) $10 + 2 =$

(19) $4 + 2 =$

(20) $16 + 2 =$

| 1 | 2 | 3 | 4 | 5 | 6 | 7 | 8 | 9 | 10 | 11 | 12 | 13 | 14 | 15 | 16 | 17 | 18 | 19 | 20 |

34 Adding 2
14+2 to 28+2

Name   Date   /   /

To parents: When your child is able to answer all the questions on this sheet correctly, please offer lots of praise.

■ Add.

(1) $15 + 2 =$

(2) $16 + 2 =$

(3) $14 + 2 =$

(4) $17 + 2 =$

(5) $18 + 2 =$

(6) $19 + 2 =$

(7) $20 + 2 =$

(8) $21 + 2 =$

(9) $22 + 2 =$

(10) $23 + 2 =$

(11) $19 + 2 =$

(12) $20 + 2 =$

(13) $22 + 2 =$

(14) $23 + 2 =$

(15) $21 + 2 =$

(16) $20 + 2 =$

(17) $22 + 2 =$

(18) $23 + 2 =$

(19) $19 + 2 =$

(20) $21 + 2 =$

| 11 | 12 | 13 | 14 | 15 | 16 | 17 | 18 | 19 | 20 | 21 | 22 | 23 | 24 | 25 | 26 | 27 | 28 | 29 | 30 |

■ Add.

(1) 21 + 2 =

(2) 19 + 2 =

(3) 20 + 2 =

(4) 22 + 2 =

(5) 23 + 2 =

(6) 24 + 2 =

(7) 25 + 2 =

(8) 26 + 2 =

(9) 27 + 2 =

(10) 28 + 2 =

(11) 24 + 2 =

(12) 26 + 2 =

(13) 27 + 2 =

(14) 25 + 2 =

(15) 28 + 2 =

(16) 26 + 2 =

(17) 24 + 2 =

(18) 25 + 2 =

(19) 27 + 2 =

(20) 28 + 2 =

| 11 | 12 | 13 | 14 | 15 | 16 | 17 | 18 | 19 | 20 | 21 | 22 | 23 | 24 | 25 | 26 | 27 | 28 | 29 | 30 |

Adding 2
19+2 to 28+2

■ Add.

(1) $19 + 2 =$

(2) $20 + 2 =$

(3) $21 + 2 =$

(4) $23 + 2 =$

(5) $22 + 2 =$

(6) $25 + 2 =$

(7) $26 + 2 =$

(8) $24 + 2 =$

(9) $27 + 2 =$

(10) $28 + 2 =$

(11) $20 + 2 =$

(12) $21 + 2 =$

(13) $19 + 2 =$

(14) $22 + 2 =$

(15) $23 + 2 =$

(16) $24 + 2 =$

(17) $26 + 2 =$

(18) $28 + 2 =$

(19) $25 + 2 =$

(20) $27 + 2 =$

| 11 | 12 | 13 | 14 | 15 | 16 | 17 | 18 | 19 | 20 | 21 | 22 | 23 | 24 | 25 | 26 | 27 | 28 | 29 | 30 |

■ Add.

(1) 20 + 2 =

(2) 23 + 2 =

(3) 27 + 2 =

(4) 21 + 2 =

(5) 24 + 2 =

(6) 28 + 2 =

(7) 19 + 2 =

(8) 25 + 2 =

(9) 22 + 2 =

(10) 26 + 2 =

(11) 22 + 2 =

(12) 26 + 2 =

(13) 24 + 2 =

(14) 19 + 2 =

(15) 25 + 2 =

(16) 21 + 2 =

(17) 20 + 2 =

(18) 27 + 2 =

(19) 23 + 2 =

(20) 28 + 2 =

| 11 | 12 | 13 | 14 | 15 | 16 | 17 | 18 | 19 | 20 | 21 | 22 | 23 | 24 | 25 | 26 | 27 | 28 | 29 | 30 |

Adding 2
1+2 to 28+2

Name   Date   / /

To parents: If your child is able to do addition easily, you may want to make some additional adding 2 problems and give them to your child.

■ Add.

(1) $1 + 2 =$

(2) $2 + 2 =$

(3) $3 + 2 =$

(4) $5 + 2 =$

(5) $6 + 2 =$

(6) $7 + 2 =$

(7) $9 + 2 =$

(8) $10 + 2 =$

(9) $11 + 2 =$

(10) $13 + 2 =$

(11) $4 + 2 =$

(12) $9 + 2 =$

(13) $8 + 2 =$

(14) $1 + 2 =$

(15) $10 + 2 =$

(16) $5 + 2 =$

(17) $12 + 2 =$

(18) $2 + 2 =$

(19) $6 + 2 =$

(20) $11 + 2 =$

1	2	3	4	5	6	7	8	9	10	11	12	13	14	15	16	17	18	19	20

■Add.

(1) 14 + 2 =

(2) 15 + 2 =

(3) 17 + 2 =

(4) 18 + 2 =

(5) 20 + 2 =

(6) 22 + 2 =

(7) 23 + 2 =

(8) 25 + 2 =

(9) 27 + 2 =

(10) 28 + 2 =

(11) 16 + 2 =

(12) 21 + 2 =

(13) 19 + 2 =

(14) 24 + 2 =

(15) 28 + 2 =

(16) 15 + 2 =

(17) 22 + 2 =

(18) 26 + 2 =

(19) 20 + 2 =

(20) 17 + 2 =

| 11 | 12 | 13 | 14 | 15 | 16 | 17 | 18 | 19 | 20 | 21 | 22 | 23 | 24 | 25 | 26 | 27 | 28 | 29 | 30 |

Review

To parents: From this page on, your child will review addition with the numbers 1 and 2. If they have difficulty, please return to previous pages for further practice.

■ Add.

(1) $1 + 1 =$

(2) $4 + 1 =$

(3) $9 + 1 =$

(4) $12 + 1 =$

(5) $15 + 1 =$

(6) $17 + 1 =$

(7) $20 + 1 =$

(8) $23 + 1 =$

(9) $24 + 1 =$

(10) $28 + 1 =$

(11) $2 + 2 =$

(12) $5 + 2 =$

(13) $8 + 2 =$

(14) $13 + 2 =$

(15) $16 + 2 =$

(16) $19 + 2 =$

(17) $21 + 2 =$

(18) $22 + 2 =$

(19) $25 + 2 =$

(20) $28 + 2 =$

■Add.

(1) $2 + 1 =$

(2) $5 + 1 =$

(3) $7 + 1 =$

(4) $11 + 1 =$

(5) $14 + 1 =$

(6) $3 + 2 =$

(7) $4 + 2 =$

(8) $9 + 2 =$

(9) $10 + 2 =$

(10) $14 + 2 =$

(11) $16 + 1 =$

(12) $18 + 1 =$

(13) $19 + 1 =$

(14) $22 + 1 =$

(15) $27 + 1 =$

(16) $15 + 2 =$

(17) $18 + 2 =$

(18) $20 + 2 =$

(19) $24 + 2 =$

(20) $26 + 2 =$

 **Review**

■ Add.

(1)　3 + 1 =

(2)　6 + 1 =

(3)　8 + 1 =

(4)　11 + 1 =

(5)　10 + 1 =

(6)　1 + 2 =

(7)　4 + 2 =

(8)　7 + 2 =

(9)　6 + 2 =

(10)　11 + 2 =

(11)　13 + 1 =

(12)　17 + 1 =

(13)　25 + 1 =

(14)　21 + 1 =

(15)　29 + 1 =

(16)　12 + 2 =

(17)　15 + 2 =

(18)　18 + 2 =

(19)　27 + 2 =

(20)　23 + 2 =

■ Add.

（1） 2 + 1 =

（2） 4 + 1 =

（3） 9 + 1 =

（4） 7 + 1 =

（5） 3 + 2 =

（6） 5 + 2 =

（7） 8 + 2 =

（8） 10 + 2 =

（9） 12 + 1 =

（10） 15 + 1 =

（11） 19 + 1 =

（12） 23 + 1 =

（13） 14 + 2 =

（14） 16 + 2 =

（15） 19 + 2 =

（16） 22 + 2 =

（17） 27 + 1 =

（18） 26 + 1 =

（19） 24 + 2 =

（20） 28 + 2 =

Review

Name

Date

/ /

To parents: When your child has finished this book, give them the Certificate of Achievement on which you can write their name and the date. Give your child lots of praise for their effort!

■ Add.

(1) 2 + 1 =

(2) 5 + 1 =

(3) 3 + 2 =

(4) 6 + 2 =

(5) 9 + 1 =

(6) 8 + 1 =

(7) 10 + 2 =

(8) 12 + 2 =

(9) 13 + 1 =

(10) 11 + 1 =

(11) 18 + 2 =

(12) 15 + 2 =

(13) 17 + 1 =

(14) 16 + 1 =

(15) 21 + 2 =

(16) 20 + 2 =

(17) 22 + 1 =

(18) 26 + 2 =

(19) 25 + 1 =

(20) 28 + 2 =

■ Add.

(1)   1 + 1 =

(2)   17 + 2 =

(3)   6 + 1 =

(4)   4 + 2 =

(5)   14 + 1 =

(6)   2 + 2 =

(7)   21 + 1 =

(8)   13 + 2 =

(9)   7 + 2 =

(10)   20 + 1 =

(11)   24 + 1 =

(12)   9 + 2 =

(13)   25 + 2 =

(14)   29 + 1 =

(15)   27 + 1 =

(16)   11 + 2 =

(17)   5 + 2 =

(18)   18 + 1 =

(19)   22 + 2 =

(20)   3 + 1 =

Certificate of Achievement

_____

is hereby congratulated on completing

My Book of Simple Addition

Presented on _____ , 20 _____

_____
Parent or Guardian

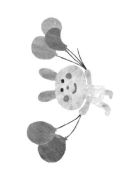

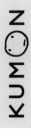

KUM◯N